The Wit and Wisdom of Denis Healey

Dr. Eileen Metcalfe

authorHOUSE®

AuthorHouse™ UK Ltd.
500 Avebury Boulevard
Central Milton Keynes, MK9 2BE
www.authorhouse.co.uk
Phone: 08001974150

First published by AuthorHouse 9/10/2007

ISBN: 978-1-4343-0361-5 (sc)

Printed in the United States of America
Bloomington, Indiana

This book is printed on acid-free paper.

I wish to thank my husband and daughter for their support and my friend Paula Eames for reading the typescript and helping to sort out the commas.

These extracts are for those who enjoy wit for its own sake.

This is an informal, lighthearted look at the wit and wisdom of some of Denis Healey's contributions to political debate made both inside and outside of the House of Commons.

The writer would like Denis Healey to be remembered for his genius with words and images.

Wit is also used here in the broader sense of wisdom and common sense, akin to the meaning in the Irish expression: "He hasn't the wit he was born with."

Denis Healey is one of the greatest and most admired politicians of his age. In his speeches, comments and answers, whether pithy or long drawn-out, he never failed to put his point across memorably, achieving stunning effect with little apparent labour.

His stand-alone, witty comments quoted here are largely self-explanatory.

These contributions are not given in chronological order but rather on the nature of their impact. Part of their interest now is that they belong to an almost forgotten age when politicians spoke with conviction and strength of feeling and not with an eye to what would bring them votes.

Many of his pithy statements and answers leave us all thinking 'I wish I had said that.'

Denis Healey was born in 1917 and brought up in Yorkshire.

He gained a double first at Balliol College, Oxford.

He joined the war, a day-one volunteer, and was a soldier for six years.

After the war he spent the following six years as International Secretary of the Labour Party which gave him opportunities to meet almost all the significant socialist leaders from around the world.

In 1952 he became a Labour Member of Parliament for Leeds and served thirty three years on Labour's Front Bench in Government and in Opposition. These included long periods as Defence Secretary, Chancellor of the Exchequer and Shadow Foreign Secretary.

He entered the House of Lords in 1992 as Lord Healey of Riddlesden.

He is one of the giants of post war politics who will be remembered for his jovial wit, his cheery arrogance, aggression in speeches, directness, his rash, rough, noisy style and, above all, for his outbursts that make politics memorable.

It has been said of him that he had a genius for calling "spades" "bloody shovels".

In political terms he was a big man in an age of giants. To get a mention from him could be viewed as a badge of honour.

He has also been described as a "stroppy West Riding Jeeves". This is the image that is portrayed here for the most part.

Aristotle said:

> "Melancholy men are, of all others, the most witty."

Denis Healey certainly does not fit this mould. He radiates good humour and a sense of well-being, the epitome of a happy man. Even when attacks on his opponents appeared brutal, the tone was one of fun and never malicious.

Dr. Johnson said:

"Everyman thinks the worse of himself for not being a soldier."

Photographs show Denis Healey as a handsome young soldier, a beach-master at Anzio for the Italian landings. Having been a soldier gave him gravitas when, even as a very young man, he confronted Churchill and Eden in the House of Commons and older colleagues at Party Conferences.

As one of the most cultured men of his age, his autobiography "The Time of My Life" is, in itself, a highly readable education in art, literature, music, politics and a who's who of the twentieth century. It ought to be compulsory reading for gifted and talented pupils in all schools.

Hansard records show Healey as a serious politician who had a deep and detailed knowledge of all the subjects he addressed in the House of Commons. However serious the nature of his speeches and replies, he could often make his points more readily understood by his native wit.

Johnson could have been describing Denis Healey when he said:

"The colloquial wit has always his own radiance reflected in himself and enjoys all the pleasures which he bestows; he finds his power confessed by everyone that approaches him, sees friendship kindling with rapture, and attention swelling into praise."

His colleagues in The House of Commons revelled in the fun and often made this obvious.

Likewise:

"The call for novelty is never satisfied, and one jest only raises expectations of another." (Johnson; Rambler)

The indulgence afforded him in the House of Commons clearly displays this kind of expectation of fun whenever he rose to speak.

A typical comment made in discussion of the Hong Kong Bill shows this appreciation from Mr. Richard Luce (The Minister of State, Foreign and Commonwealth Office):

"Nevertheless, there was a not uncharacteristic music hall knock-about performance from the right hon. Member for Leeds East (Mr. Healey) who seemed to be enjoying himself for the first 10 or 15 minutes….. when he talks about the Prime Minister I always enjoy myself. The right hon. Member for Leeds East can talk about tigers and elephants to his heart's content……"

Lord Chesterfield said:

"Wit is so shining a quality that everybody admires it; most people aim at it, all people fear it, and few love it unless in themselves. A man must have a good share of wit himself to endure a great share of it in another."

This goes for women too. Mrs. Thatcher endured a lot, with little retaliation. She probably enjoyed the attention and knew only too well when to deny her opponents the pleasure of her discomfort. Also, there is no such thing as bad publicity.

Emerson said:

"Wit makes its own welcome, and levels all distinctions. No dignity, no learning, no force of character can make any stand against a good wit."

This is what I hope to reveal here. Also, Healey's banter enlivened the dullness of the House of Commons.

The first words on Healey as a parliamentarian were when he was complimented by Fitzroy MacLean, a war hero,

"… a most remarkable maiden speech, speaking his own words now not as in the past by others, backroom boys – emerged as an orator in his own right and an outstanding orator at that."

The depth and detail in his speeches show him to be The Labour Party's in-house intellectual, intriguing because he could be both elegant and brutal".

From his early days Healey was not afraid to take on the senior members of all parties in parliament and in the powerful Unions.

At the 1952 Conference in Morecambe the young Denis Healey drummed up laughter with the following comment about his senior Labour colleagues:

> "…but now we know that the only difference between Nye Bevan and Herbert Morrison is that Nye thinks that the best way to win friends and influence people is to kick them in the teeth. That is a point of view, but I believe that even in the country of Humphrey Bogart and James Cagney, they do not understand that kind of lovemaking."

Also in 1952 he showed self assurance with this jovial observation on French/German rivalry.

Referring to the re-armament and control of Germany, Healey, catching Eden's re-action to his words, said:

> "I see the Foreign Secretary pursing his lips. He is right. That prospect dismays the French."

He took on enemies within the Labour Party and could fell effectively with a single blow.

On open-ended borrowing and industrial protection he said:

> "I will say one thing: I do not want to be lectured by any member of our movement on the need for import controls when they ask their own trade unions to provide them with a Volvo."

In similar vein he warns:

> "No election would be won if we go on ideological ego trips or accept the clapped out dogmas which are now being trailed by the toy-town Trotskyists of the Militant group."

Speaking against RA Butler on disengagement or otherwise from Africa, Healey says:

> "One of the things we most admire about the right hon. Gentleman is his ability to sidle off in opposite directions at the same time without any apparent feeling of

inconsistency. I know that he is a man of flesh and blood, but in his political career he gives the impression of being made of ectoplasm."

And now among friends:

Healey called Richard Crossman "a Machiavelli without judgement."

Crossman thought Denis Healey was a very lone mover, completely on his own, running his own ideas. This illustrates his power and magnetism. He was a politician like no other.

Crossman also found the Prime Minister, Wilson, "full of the wickedness of Denis Healey." Healey never lost the impishness of a schoolboy.

Not without reason, in 1963, Crossman said of Healey- "a rather adventurous young man who sensationalizes everything".

He was identified correctly as a heavyweight even as a young man by the political correspondent, left winger Tom Driberg, who said:

> "On the back benches two young men have confirmed their quality, Denis Healey and Anthony Wedgwood Benn."

With his judicious choice of words, some of Healey's points seem as relevant now as in the 1964 election, such as:

> "The Conservatives tell us that we can never be great again unless we go cap in hand to the Americans to get atomic weapons on the hire purchase system. Have we really sunk so low? We believe that greatness cannot be bought from foreigners on the instalment plan. It is something we must do by our own efforts."

He was aware of social and political correctness before these concepts were born within politics.

As a young MP in 1953 he was not afraid to give the Prime Minister, Winston Churchill, a rollicking. In a debate on the Far East situation after pointing out how the Prime Minister misled Congress in the U.S. he goes on:

> "Personally, I am glad at least that this time the Prime Minister's visit was a private one, because on this occasion he was able only to mislead Mr. Eisenhower and Mr. Dulles and not the American people…...I do not think that the right

atmosphere for such consultations is the atmosphere of rather pompous patronage, talking to erring schoolboys such as was recommended by the right hon. Member for Haltemprice, (Mr. Law) in which the peculiar characteristics of the genus 'American' is analysed in public as if talking about 'the African' in the nineteenth century."

Later that year in a debate on foreign affairs he pointed to some significant hot spots that were going to be etched for ever on our consciousness:

"I could not help avoiding the feeling when I read the Prime Minister's (Churchill's) speech - I was in Strasbourg at the time - that he was hankering after the great days of Yalta and Teheran, when a few men, of whom he was one, sliced up the world into spheres of influence in an orgy of power politics. That proceeding was both possible and necessary.......in the present situation it is neither possible nor necessary.......There are now other countries which can think and act for themselves in Europe, in the Middle East and in Asia."

In 1954 in a foreign affairs debate he says with some roguishness:

"No one can blame a Foreign Secretary for confining himself largely to platitudes when he makes statements about delicate diplomatic problems. Indeed, I think that when foreign secretaries diverge from platitudes, they sometimes do more harm than good."

On the Foreign Secretary (Anthony Eden) being hampered by the Prime Minister he says:

"The Prime Minister (Churchill), particularly this year, has confined his speeches largely to scattering a number of thunder flashes which dazzle the audience for a moment and then leave it shrouded in smoke for months to follow. But, of course, we have to live with this situation. If the Japanese have learned to live with earthquakes and the Italian peasant can live happily on the slopes of Vesuvius, I see no reason why a British Foreign Secretary should not survive under the leadership of the present Prime Minister."

Speaking up for the troops returning from the war:

In 1945 he said that Churchill "has insulted the intelligence and violated the confidence of the forces – the results of the policy of removal of controls in Italy where only one tenth of the people's basic needs were rationed and the other nine tenths were bought by rich and poor alike on the black market at soaring prices" ....the cost of living, he said, increased a hundred times since 1939.

He was always able and willing to champion the cause of the poorest with direct language that enabled him to get his point across clearly.

Fearing that nothing would be done to ensure work and security for the returning forces after the war he says that the Conservative plot was the same as it had always been:

"....to let the men come back, spend five or six months looking for homes and living on their gratuities and then drop back on the dole and live in a hovel or a gutter until there happened to be some work in the area."

On Harold Macmillan's change of mind (1958):

"We know the right hon. Gentleman's versatility as a quick-change artist too well to take his posture from time to time as clear evidence of what he is really thinking."

Again in 1960 he attacks Macmillan's lack of constructive leadership and dependence on favours from the Pentagon in his:

"….faltering speech, full of soggy platitudes, with no bite or precision. He seemed dazed himself when he began it, and he had us all dazed when he sat down."

He continues:

"The Prime Minister this afternoon had the ball at his feet, but he simply touched it tentatively with his toe and then shuffled sleepily off the field."

In 1968 in one of his many confrontations with Enoch Powell he shows how to debunk an officious opponent:

"I was told to resign last week by the right hon. Member for Wolverhampton South West (Mr. Powell) in a performance positively manic in intensity …..The trouble is that we have heard it all before. The right hon. Gentleman has told me to resign every time he has spoken as the Shadow Minister of Defence. The right hon. Gentleman was particularly ferocious last week because he was defending his party's undertaking to stay on in the Far East after 1971……..He obviously thought that if he shrieked loud enough and made a lot of nasty faces no one would notice that he was standing on his head."

Again on Enoch Powell, damning with faint praise:

"I do not object to the right hon. Member for Wolverhampton South West coming to the fray laden with faded Defence White Papers, old copies of Hansard, yellowing newspaper cuttings and transcripts of television programmes."

In May '75 in a debate on the economy he used a similar attack on the opposition:

"All we had was a monotonous recitation of disconnected little homilies on each of the economic abstractions, studded with indigestible quotations from the whole gamut of Tory house journals from The Sunday Telegraph to The Economist and charged with all the moral passion and intellectual distinction of a railway time-table."

Commenting on the Conservative Government's continuous series of somersaults on defence policy he says:

"They invented a brilliant technique. They switched their Defence Minister to another job before the somersaults took place. That is why they had nine Defence Ministers in thirteen years and why our defences were in such a mess in 1964. ....There we have it - nine Defence Ministers in thirteen years, one long stream of somersaults in policy......The only obvious concern of those Defence ministers was not to be found holding the baby when the music stopped. They institutionalized passing the buck as part of the machinery of Conservative Government."

On the purpose of nuclear defence:

As always, his approach was "let's get it clear." On nuclear defence he stated that Sir Alec Douglas-Home reverted to "a purely nuclear strategy of what he calls a trip wire which trips" and his assertion that a trip wire will gain hours, perhaps days or a week. Healey responds:

> "If the right hon. Gentleman has ever talked to a poacher, he will know that the function of a trip wire is not to trip but to kill."

In 1971, injecting a note of common sense into an extended debate on the European Economic Community he said:

> "The Common Market is often described as a cold shower which will bring our industries into a more healthy state

of mind. But a cold shower which is bracing to a healthy man can be fatal to a man suffering from diabetes or tuberculosis."

Further, commenting on Enoch Powell's (Wolverhampton) fears about the loss of freedoms such as sovereignty within the EEC he says:

"Having dazzled us with a display of pure reason, he then appealed to the dark instincts of primeval blood and earth. This is a style of his – beating the ideological tom-tom – with which we are all familiar, and it never fails to assemble the tribes."

Continuing the theme on the degree of national sovereignty we have in the EEC he says:

"Britain is not a suburb of Wolverhampton spinning through outer space and separated by a million light years from all other human kind. Britain is part of an international community which has shrunk enormously in our lifetime."

He then points out Britain's contacts, commitments, diplomacy, economy, defence and demand for oil.

Sometimes a few words were enough to lighten the tone yet make impact on a point.

On Mr. Rippon, Chancellor of the Duchy and in charge of EEC negotiations, he says:

> "First, I should like to ask whether the right hon. and learned Gentleman is aware that many of us feel that he might have got an acceptable and bankable agreement on sugar if he had stuck to the line he took on Tuesday night, when he talked of figures and quantities, instead of collapsing like a pricked balloon when asked to create a pleasant climate for the meeting of the Prime Minister and President Pompidou."

On the European Communities Bill an unnecessary interjection by Mr. Rippon is answered:

> "I am grateful for the right hon. and learned Gentleman's interjection. I do not know

whether he has been awake for the last half-hour. If he has he will know that we are discussing precisely what may happen in the future and how the House will handle the proposals that the Community should be extended and enlarged so as to cover defence, as the right hon. and Learned Gentleman himself suggested it might do in the question to which I have referred."

Regarding The Common Market, Oct 1971, he argues that the member countries of the Six did not grow faster by joining the Common Market:

"Yesterday The Financial Times leader, in an excess of euphoria, said that by joining the Common Market we would get higher growth, longer holidays, a shorter working week and bigger social services - everything except free beer and champagne …."

In 1955 he is wary of the Russians beginning to appear more agreeable.

He says the burglar might be offering "to return a small part of his loot only on condition that he receives something of the same value in exchange."

On restrictions in use of Parliamentary language in The House of Commons:

He attacked Anthony Eden's statement that he had consulted the US and the Commonwealth governments over his response to Suez when Healey maintained that they had not been consulted. He concluded:

> "Mr. Speaker: Could you please tell me what is the Parliamentary expression which comes closest to expressing the meaning of the word 'liar'."

Much later, in 1987 he asks:

> "What is the parliamentary word for tripe? There must be something suitable."

Similarly, tongue in cheek, pointing up the requirement to speak with decorum but at the same time stretching tolerance to the limits, he says on NATO Council (Ministerial Meeting):

> "First there was the furtive, shifty and muddled handling of the planned move of the American headquarters from Germany

to Britain. I choose my words carefully, out of deference to parliamentary procedure."

In 1975 Healey was rebuked for the use of un-parliamentary language when Mr. Peyton complained on a point of order:

"The Chancellor of The Exchequer was heard distinctly to use the words 'bloody humbug'."

The Speaker calls for order saying that the Minister is out of order.

"If the words were applied to an argument, I deprecate the epithet very much. The noun is not out of order."

Healey answers: "I withdraw the word bloody and substitute revolting."

When required to apologise to Mr. Biffen he said:

"I apologise to the right hon. Gentleman. I shall replace the word contempt with distaste and mistrust."

He congratulated Eden on standing up to his 'dinosaurs and Teddy boys' when he made it clear that the solution to Suez was interaction and striving for consent. He points to Eden's reputation as a soft touch with a snappy finale:

> "Let us not make a sort of Chauvinistic hullabaloo which only encourages other countries to twist the lion's tail. There is no pastime more attractive than twisting the lion's tail if one knows it will make him roar and is almost sure that it will not make him bite."

On the Suez crisis:

From his position on the shadow front bench he unleashed a wave of facts with dramatic simplicity, observing that "our policy has somersaulted at least twice a year and in the last year four times". Healey was a foreign affairs specialist and knew how to use simple statistics for maximum effect.

He says of Mr. Khrushchev

> "….as he indicated in his own words recently, he proposes to make the Western

Governments jump about like fish in a frying pan."

Later he quoted Khrushchev again adding:

"I only wish that he could get it into his head that one cannot negotiate disarmament or anything else with fish in a frying pan, particularly if one is holding them over the fire oneself."

On Communism, words of wisdom that are still relevant

"The idea that Soviet Communism is the cause of all the trouble in the modern world is just as ridiculous as its mirror image – the view of infantile pseudo Marxists that all the trouble in the world is caused by capitalism. The world suffered from wars and revolutions for at least two thousand years before the Spinning Jenny was invented or the Bolsheviks stormed the Winter Palace. To attribute all the complex problems of the world....... to this comic strip interpretation which President Regan undoubtedly genuinely believes is profoundly dangerous to world peace."

The Conservatives often alluded to his communist days, probably in the hope of frightening the electorate. Some of the best attacks on Healey were in Healey's own style, as follows:

Geoffrey Ripon (Hexham) said that a Commonwealth Prime Minister had said of Denis Healey that:

> "…he has the best trained Marxist mind in the Western world", and then continued….
> "His casuistry is marvellous. If the right hon. Gentleman went to work on a bicycle he would ride it vigorously in one direction and then turn around in front of one's very eyes and say 'I am still going in the same direction.' Sometimes he speaks with such authority that people are apt to believe that he pursues a consistent purpose."

Healey, who could always get his man, replies:

> "I am fascinated that the right hon. and learned Gentleman finds it so difficult to deal with any of the points I made that he must go in for the trumpery of character assassination. But whose character is he assassinating? He began by saying that I had

been an absolutely consistent agent of the Soviet Union for the last 30 years and the next moment he said that I change direction every few days. Can he help on that?"

In his student Communist days he says that one of the favourite topics for discussion was: ".... 'Who will do the dirty work under socialism?' In later life I discovered that the answer was Denis Healey."

In 1971, commenting on improved links between the West, Russia and China and in particular on President Nixon's visit to Peking, Secretary Brezhnev's visit to France and Prime Minister Kosygin's visit to Canada he says:

"Indeed anyone who reads the newspapers to-day must imagine that both Joseph Stalin and Foster Dulles are spinning in their graves."

On spies, in a Foreign Affairs debate (1971), there are shades of 'Our Man in Havana':

"Spies are a product of political conflict. All countries try to keep some things secret, and their political enemies try to find them out. There is no doubt in my mind that the KGB is the biggest feather-bedded industry in the world, that thousands of Soviet KGB men spend money painfully collected from Russian workers to have a wonderful time in foreign countries, largely collecting information which could be collected as easily and much faster by a girl with scissors and a pile of newspapers in Moscow."

On the fall of Communism:

An astute politician, he foresaw that the fall of communism would bring problems, with these prophetic words:

> "….. when Tito dies, and he will some day, there might be the possibility of civil war inside Yugoslavia and of outside intervention."

Perhaps not quite what Lenin meant:

In 1991 he says: "Lenin, who does not often get a kind word these days, was right in at least one of his prophesies. He prophesied that the triumph of communism would lead to the withering away of the state. I do not think that anyone has ever seen a state wither away quite as fast as the Soviet state has in recent weeks."

People are flattered by the personal touch.

Until he became a Cabinet Minister in 1964, he was earning a thousand a year with no allowance for a secretary so he wrote all his letters by hand out of necessity. This, he says, was much appreciated by his constituents who attributed it to principle rather than penury. With characteristic wit and a good measure of truth he says that Members of Parliament were treated "…like middle-ranking civil servants which is probably the best compromise available for an occupation which accommodates the extremes of overwork and idleness."

He was a past-master in the art of engendering a robust debate and could carry on regardless.

In 1966 with an impending election he says:

> "I thought that we had a first rate knockabout speech from the right hon. Member for Barnet (Mr. Maudling), and I

imagine that after the election many of his hon. and right hon. friends will be putting up the sticker 'Don't blame me, I voted Maudling'. It is worthwhile if we are to treat this problem with the seriousness it deserves. (Hon Members: "Oh!") Please let me get on (interruption), I was interrupted forty times in my speech yesterday, and I do not propose to be deflected from answering questions which have been put to me."

He could always control the many interruptions to his speeches as follows:

"I have a duty to the House to make these points and I remind the hon. Gentlemen opposite that it is no good their complaining that they do not get the facts if they prevent me from giving them by behaving like a lot of schoolboys."

"I shall give way from time to time, but I do not wish to conduct a seminar."

Or:

"As I was saying before I was so agreeably interrupted I cannot forecast...."

Answering the many interruptions by Rear Admiral Morgan in a debate on Rhodesia:

> "The hon. and gallant Gentleman gives a very good imitation of a jack in the box, but his interventions add very little to our proceedings."

However, there was no repressing his own blithe spirit when refused permission to intervene.

He makes another effort:

> "May I intervene for a moment as pithecanthropus erectus?"

In 1966, on Britain's role overseas

He made impact with a serious voice on Britain's momentous disengagement from imperial rule and withdrawals to be made from East of Suez. He says that events "....have brought fully home to the House that this is the end of two centuries of British history, an era which covers some of the brightest pages and some of the darkest, in the story of our people".

In similar vein 1968 he said:

"Disengagement from the empire, as we all know, is always difficult and painful especially when it is reluctant."

He was adept at capturing the essence of the personal characteristics of politicians.

Throughout January 1974 when Edward Heath was dithering on whether or not to call an election Healey told the house:

"….there is an element of stony rigidity in his makeup which tends to petrify his whole personality in a crisis. He should never have allowed himself to be manipulated into a dead end by an oddly assorted quartet of his colleagues, who are now trundling him like a great marble statue towards the precipice."

On Mr. Heath's censure on the Minister of Aviation, Healey says cheekily:

"On a point of order, Mr. Speaker. May I have a little guidance? I am not quite clear whether the right hon. Gentleman is interrupting before I sit down or whether he is making a speech."

Brevity is the soul of wit. (Shakespeare)

In his memoirs Healey compares Tony Benn with Stafford Cripps......"a political ninny of the most superior quality".

Speaking of George Wigg he says: "I cannot say my heart always rose when his long ant-eater's proboscis began to quiver, and his mouth began its gobbling splutter."

Montgomery: "A sharp ferret-blue face, thin lipped mouth and very pale grey-green eyes."

Harold Laski: a "mousey little man – his warm heart and big sorrowful eyes…"

As to the right time to act, he says:

> "You do not conduct an appendix operation on a man while he is moving a grand piano on the stairs."

On economics: He described economic forecasting as "extrapolation from a partially known past, through an unknown present, to an unknowable future…."

He says that the argument about who won at Maastricht is "pitifully irrelevant".

In a debate on pay and prices he picks up Mr. Pardoe's reference to 'pathetic' replying: "I always defer to the hon. Gentleman's experience when he refers to the pathetic."

A comment to Timothy Raison, the Minister for Overseas Development: "Baloney."

On sanctions against Poland he responds to Mr. Rifkind:

"Bullshit!"

Mr Rifkind responds in a typical Denis Healey manner:

"That is a very reasoned response – one that is slightly superior to the right hon. Gentleman's earlier comments."

Response to a budget debate:

"It is another enormous dose of a medicine that has made the patient as sick as a dog."(79/80)

The elder Kerolyi: "gaga but impressive, with a queer mumbling palatial speech."

Reisz: "… as usual the general ruffian".

"Fighting men recognize Goebbels even when he smokes a cigar."

Healey, always a man of the people, points out that

"The Inland Revenue saw themselves strictly as laying down the law to a nation of natural tax-dodgers."

Still relevant today

- commenting on the Armed Forces' pay rise and the feeling in the Services that what is given by the Ministry of Defence is taken away in tax, Healey comments that it is vitally important that this should be remedied saying: "I am conscious that no one in the Services is interested in what I believe is known as an Irishman's rise."

He uses the visual well to introduce chummy moments:

"I note that the right hon. Member for Blaby (Mr. Lawson) shakes his head." Healey then continues with an example of increased interest rates and ERM. "I am glad to see that the right hon. Gentleman is now nodding in agreement."

In 1983: "I am glad that the new Under Secretary of State at the ForeignOffice is nodding his head. I presume that it was in agreement with me, because he showed no signs whatever of exhaustion."

Even his general comments had an innate dramatic flourish:

He thought the chaplain "an obvious inoffensive fool, talking about himself as 'a bloke who wears a back to front collar' and was clearly waiting for Alan Bennett."

He could always correct the careless use of words:

"It is true as he said that there was no legal impediment to unions which wished to do so protecting their funds by hiving them off and registering as friendly societies. There are, of course, no legal difficulties in the way of the right hon. Gentleman living on the moon but in practice the difficulties in both cases are formidable."

In his memoirs he tells how on a visit to the Middle East as Defence Secretary he delighted the sheiks in the mountains surrounding Aden with the story of the frog and the scorpion:

"A frog was sunning himself on the bank of the river Nile when a scorpion walked up and asked for a lift across the river.

'No fear', said the frog, 'if you get on my back you'll sting me and I'll die.'

'Nonsense' replied the scorpion, 'if you die, I'll drown.'

The frog thought it over and agreed. The scorpion got on his back and the frog plopped into the river. When they were exactly half way across, the frog felt an agonizing pain between his shoulder blades and realized he had been stung.

'Why did you do it?' he asked as his limbs began to stiffen. 'You know you'll drown.'

'Yes, I know, replied the scorpion. But after all this is the Middle East'."

Healey acknowledges his Irish roots.

As Defence Secretary he was Mountbatten's boss. When he demoted Mountbatten he was told that some of his penniless Irish relations, whom he had never met, and who lived in peat huts outside Mountbatten's castle at Classiebawn, were delighted to know that Healey was Mountbatten's boss. (Incidentally, peat huts had disappeared from the Irish scene long before this period.)

When lecturing at the Services Colleges in the years before becoming Defence Secretary and when explaining what he was trying to do he used to compare himself with an Indian chief who called his braves together at the outset of winter and said: "I have two bits of news for you - one bad, the other good. First, the bad news: There's going to be nothing to eat this winter except buffalo shit. Now, the good news: There's going to be plenty of buffalo shit around."

This, he says, was generally well received until, on one occasion, he discovered it had been told earlier by someone else.

Edna Healey, in her book 'Part of the Pattern', says that he always joked that he could say in every language, "In the name of the

Labour Party I wish you a successful congress" and "I love you beautiful lady" – but that he had to take care not to confuse them.

He used to compare Nigel Lawson, in his earlier years at the Treasury, with the driver who was stopped by the police on a motorway.

The driver wound down his window to be told he was drunk. "Thank God," he replied "I thought the steering had gone."

How we wish we had him around to-day to give an update on the present state of taxation.

On the inequalities of tax in 1972 Healey uses a simple illustration effectively, showing his true Labour credentials.

On tax levies in a Conservative Finance Bill, especially the ten percent tax on children's clothes and shoes he says:

> "The concept of 'one nation' does not consist of forcing the working class child to walk to school in ill fitting shoes while the millionaire rides to his office in a Rolls-Royce paid for out of tax by his own

business or, if he bought it himself, bought on hire purchase at the effective interest rate of one and a half percent."

Again on tax, nothing has changed since he said in 1972 that……..

"….in their present form the VAT proposals are a feast for fiddlers and form fillers; they are expensive and inefficient; they are crammed with anomalies and are an invitation to evasion."

He illustrates one example well and with a hint of fun, for example, the tax on the fried potato:

"If we fry it at home it attracts no VAT. If someone else fries it for us in a restaurant, it attracts 10 per cent VAT. If someone fries it for us in a fish and chip shop it attracts no VAT if we eat it outside the shop but 10 per cent VAT if we eat it in the shop. To further this quintessence of idiocy, if this fried potato is cold and served in a sealed packet, it attracts 10 per cent VAT whether we eat it at home or in the shop where we buy it. We still have to wait for some Minister to enlighten us on the question put by my hon. Friend, the Member for Heywood and Royston, on the Second Reading, as to how many chips we have to eat between the counter and the door in order to be relieved of how much VAT in a fish and chip shop."

After a long and detailed debate on the Budget in 1973 Healey asks and then answers:

"What does that mean in plain language? It means that the whole burden of paying for the Government's Budget, of paying for the balance-of-payments gap and for the consequence of devaluation, is to be thrown on to the working man and his wife."

On the Heath Government in November 1973 he again simplifies a huge problem in memorable words:

"Last week 332 new price increases were announced, bringing the total since the last General Election to over 30,000. We were told by a Treasury

Minister last week that the pound has now sunk to 77p in value compared with its value at the time of the General Election."

Later he asks provocatively:

"....however, can the hon. Gentleman assure the House that he will fight the next election on the slogan: 'Another three years of the Tory Government and the £ will be worth only 50p'?"

Later in 1974 when challenged by Mr. Heath to tell the House about the rises in petrol, Healey responded to Heath's rather histrionic speech:

"I do not think that it would be right for me to interrupt the right hon. Gentleman's first electioneering speech."

True wit is nature to advantage dressed, What oft was thought, but ne'er so well expressed. (Alexander Pope)

This sentiment pervades all Denis Healey's words.

Drawing attention to the con tricks of advertising that we have not yet fully addressed, Healey gives a good lead, as follows, on the use of Saatchi and Saatchi advertising by the Conservatives.

In a debate on the economic situation in June 1978 he pointed out:

> "The fact is that the Opposition have not the slightest idea what policies they would follow on tax or public expenditure or anything else. They have already abandoned policy as an element in their appeal to the British people. They rely instead on an advertising agency called Saatchi and Saatchi to market them by the same techniques as is used for marketing Penguin biscuits, Quality Street chocolates, Fairy Snow and, appropriately, Schhh…. You know who."

Later, in November 1978, he comments again on one of Saatchi and Saatchi's techniques:

> "Then we get Saatchi and Saatchi producing a queue of unemployed who turn out to be not real unemployed but layabouts

from North Hendon Conservative Association."

He then has a bit of fun pointing out another advertising trick:

"We had one of the most delightful episodes in recent political history – the saga of Sarah Cramp. I quote from the Daily Mail: "Pensioner Sarah Cramp revealed today how she was tricked into playing the part of a hard up widow called Annie for a Conservative Party Political broadcast….Mrs. Cramp said today: 'that was all nonsense. The film crew deceived me…..I don't blame the Labour Government for inflation. And if the Labour Party asked me to do a film for them I would agree."

Healey adds: "I can understand the dismay of the Conservatives at the thought of all that money pouring down the drain."

"Wit is more often a shield than a lance" (Anon.):

One of his best remembered jokes was, in fact, used as a shield.

As Chancellor of the Exchequer listening to the considered response of the Opposition's Shadow Chancellor, Sir Geoffrey Howe, he says in his autobiography that in one debate Howe had raised some difficult questions in his opening speech. Healey did not want to be distracted from his own argument by answering them, so he dismissed them by saying that he found Geoffrey Howe's attack "rather like being savaged by a dead sheep". He says the phrase came to him while he was actually on his feet; it was an adaptation of Churchill's remark that an attack by Attlee was "like being savaged by a pet lamb".

Geoffrey Howe was a favourite target.

In 1984, on nuclear weapons, he says:

> "Europe cannot afford to wait until the United States has sorted out its familiar muddles. I was pleased by one suggestion apparently made by the Foreign Secretary. I hope that I did not misunderstand him. Searching in the bran tub of his woolly rhetoric for the nuggets of meaning is sometimes a tiring and exhausting job. However, the Foreign Secretary seems to suggest that Britain should lead in this area. I strongly agree with him."

In 1985 he says: "May I congratulate the Foreign Secretary on the penetrating and comprehensive critique of the Star Wars programme that he made the other day, and on provoking an alarming outburst of hysteria from the editor of The Times."

In 1987, "In the right hon. and learned Gentleman's new capacity as pedlar of lodestones of guidance, does he believe that it would be wise for the Community to take a much more public and consistent line on the major issue of arms control?"

Some of his most memorable comments have been about Mrs. Thatcher.

In the early days of her reign he called her: "Ted Heath in drag".

However, he was not poking fun at the feeble when he chose Mrs. Thatcher; there would have been no wit in that. Perhaps he knew instinctively when he had met another giant. It would have been fun sparring with her had she retaliated.

In a speech on the economy he accused Mrs. Thatcher of "dragging a red-hot rake through the Midlands."

A Conservative attack on the unions unleashed a merry mélange of fun. When it was proposed that the information and intelligence station at GCHQ should be closed down, despite being an inoffensive and non-closed shop establishment, Healey castigated Geoffrey Howe and then burst into a typical attack on Mrs. Thatcher:

> "The foreign Secretary is not the villain in this case; he is the fall guy ...... Who is the Mephistopheles behind this shabby Faust? The handling of this decision by – I quote her own backbenchers - the Great She Elephant, She who Must Be Obeyed, the Catherine the Great of Finchley, the Prime Minister herself......The Prime Minister, for whom I have great personal affection, has formidable qualities - a powerful intelligence and great courage - but these qualities can turn into horrendous vices, unless they are moderated by colleagues who have more experience, understanding and sensitivity......I put it to the Government Front Bench that to allow the right hon. Lady to commit Britain to another four years of capricious autocracy would be to do fearful damage

not just to the Conservative Party but to the state."

Later, when his wife upbraided him for expressing affection for Mrs. Thatcher he called this "careless charity". However, as shown later, he had more true charity than he cared to admit.

In exploiting an error by Mrs. Thatcher he was in his element:

"The Prime Minister even re-wrote the whole of British history by telling the French this week that they should not be so proud of liberty, equality and fraternity because we first introduced it in Magna Carta. I learnt some history when I was a little boy. My impression was that Magna Carta had been imposed on a wicked British king by the Barons. It brought no freedom to the ordinary people of our country. If the ideals of liberty, equality and fraternity existed before the age of enlightenment in eighteenth century France, I suppose they existed among some members of the Roundhead group in the English civil war, notably the Levellers."

Among his descriptions of Mrs. Thatcher are: The Iron Lady, Attila the Hen, Britain's De Gaulle and Rhoda the Rhino.

In 1987, on Mr. Gorbachev's speech meeting an avalanche of negative briefing Healey says it emanated thus:

> "I understand from No. 10 Downing Street, which culminated in the extraordinary performance of the Prime Minister at Question Time last Thursday, when she brought the dinosaurs on her Back Benches shambling out of their caves to great approval of what she said because they thought she was taking a bold negative posture, as against the wet, wimpish posture of the American President...."

Continuing a serious discussion on Intermediate Nuclear weapons Healey says:

> "Yet ..... The Foreign Secretary took exactly the opposite view. I am glad to see that the Secretary of State for Defence agreed with him rather than the Prime Minister; I do not suppose that he is looking forward to his next meeting with Attila the Hen."

In the Falklands war, he accuses Mrs. Thatcher of not informing the Argentinean Leader, Galtieri, that she had sent seven warships off from Gibraltar to be part of a larger force saying:

> "She took no steps whatever to warn the Argentine Government......, she made no contact with them at all. She merely rang her friend President Reagan, who at some stage telephoned President Galtieri....... The President (Reagan) stated forcefully that action against the Falklands would be regarded by the British as a 'casus belli'."

Healey says that it was not wise to entrust President Reagan with that phrase. He adds that we do not know whether or not, at his end, President Galtieri understood it.

In July 1989 he says of Mrs. Thatcher:

> "During the last year the right hon. Lady has met every challenge by insulting all her allies simultaneously. She has accused President Kohl and Mr. Genscher of 'wriggling' after the last NATO summit. She insulted President Mitterand repeatedly at some press conference...... Although she has not yet told us so, it

is quite clear that she regards President Bush as an upper class wimp, so wet that one could shoot snipe off him. However, it has not helped Britain, or even the Prime Minister, to add the diplomacy of Alf Garnett to the economics of Arthur Daley. However, that is the twin blessing that she has showered on us in recent years."

He says it is possible to sympathize with Mao's theory of permanent revolution; Mao argued: "....if you don't constantly sharpen your knife it will rust."

Healey says this is a maxim Mrs. Thatcher would endorse.

Again in 1980: "What I find a little surprising about the Prime Minister is that she is terribly keen on secret ballots in the trade union movement. I wonder if she would dare to face a secret ballot of her own party to-night."

On the Hong Kong Bill (1985) amid a detailed and complex debate he says: "I hope the Foreign Secretary will assure us that in future he will not allow the Prime Minister to go on barging about like Rhoda the Rhino with her usual arrogant incompetence on issues which clearly she does not understand."

In the next breath he continues:

> "I have often expressed my qualified admiration for the Prime Minister. She has some qualities unique in her Government. There is no member of her Cabinet with whom I would rather go tiger shooting, but I should absolutely insist that, before we set out together, she was taught the difference between a tiger and an elephant – particularly the elephant that I was riding."

In his attacks on Mrs. Thatcher, Denis Healey had always something of the mischievous schoolboy humour reminding us of a bright little schoolgirl's comment on television that "boys shouldn't be allowed".

"Wit is the sudden marriage of ideas which, before their union, were not perceived to have any relation" – (Mark Twain).

Healey was a past- master of this kind of humour, using it effectively against all manner of politicians.

The following are perhaps the best remembered of Healey's outbursts on Mrs. Thatcher; they capture well the confident, strident, swashbuckling Mrs. Thatcher in her prime:

> "I was not in the least surprised the other day to see that President Giscard d'Estaing and Chancellor Schmidt saw her as a rhinoceros – an image, I may say, a great deal more appropriate to her than to her jovial companions sitting on her right, the right hon. Member for Lowestoft. (Mr. Prior) She has an impenetrable, thick hide, she is liable to mad charges in all directions and she always thinks on the trot."

Continuing the theme of the rhinoceros at a later date (May 1981) he also adds a pen picture of Sir Ian Gilmour:

> "I know the right hon. Gentleman can see why Chancellor Schmidt and even President Giscard d'Estaing refer to the Prime Minister as a rhinoceros. I mentioned this fact when I was Shadow Chancellor. What has struck me is that the Foreign Secretary (Lord Carrington) seems to be her zookeeper. He is dragged

away continually from the delicate diplomatic task of feeding the marmosets by the news that Rhoda the Rhino is on the rampage again. The poor fellow has to put down his pipette, or whatever it is that one uses to feed marmosets, and follow a trail of wrecked cars, shattered shop windows and bent lampposts, until he finally tracks her down in the middle of some great store where the counters are overturned, the goods are strewn over the floor and the sales staff are clinging to the tops of pillars. I must pay the Foreign Secretary some credit. By some magic or pitchfork, he manages to lead her back to her pen, past the flamingo pool where the Lord Privy Seal (the urbane Sir Ian Gilmour) is standing immobile, elegant and elongated, his leg in the water, pink and wet as we have always known him."

Again in October 1988

"The prime Minister has just gone to the Commonwealth Conference in Nassau in her most Rhoda-the-Rhino mood, perhaps it would be more up to date to describe her as Rambona. Once again, as

on Rhodesia, on Hong Kong and during
the talks with the Government of Eire,
she has painted herself into a corner and
relied on the Foreign Secretary to carry
her out - a heavy burden for him to carry.
In Canada, the other day, I noticed that
her faithful St. Bernard (Sir Bernard
Ingham) - the Prime Minister's official
press spokesman at Nassau - told the press
there 'We're used to being shot at. We're
riddled with the bullets of isolation. We
survive and enjoy it.'

He is a true servant of his mistress."

In July 1985: "I congratulate the right hon. and
learned Gentleman on the dogged pragmatism
with which he once again swept up the debris
caused by the eruption of Krakatoa Kate in
Milan."

Always able to entertain and capable of picking up his opponent's slightest slip:

"I am being daring in making the
suggestion in the presence of the right
hon. Lady's two loyal advocates.....
would it not be a good idea to let the
foreign secretary run British foreign

policy and to give the Foreign Office a look in? The Box is strangely depleted now and I suspect that that is because three of the civil servants have gone out to divide Das Kapital into sections and to find out which particular section justifies the Prime Minister in describing the European Community's Social Chapter as a Marxist document."

On Mrs. Thatcher's co-operation with the Republic of Eire in trying to create a framework in which it would be easier to deal with the problems of Northern Ireland, Healey says:

"But her love affair with Mr.Haughey seems to be one of the shortest in recorded history."

On several occasions he was gracious to Mrs. Thatcher over her handling of the Falklands affair but on Mrs. Thatcher's not making full use of professional advisers in the Foreign Office he says:

"Her general motto seems to be, as it always is, 'Please do not confuse me with the facts'."

And again: "….Recently the Foreign Office has moved into the firing line. For the last few months the Prime Minister has been barging about like some bargain basement Boadicea leaving dismay and disruption wherever she goes from Peking to Berlin. Thank God she has not yet gone to Gibraltar.

Finally, may I tell him that the opposition are sick and tired of the bargain -basement Boadicea barging in yet again with an off-the-cuff dismissal of Mr. Andropov's proposals ……."

> "Now the Prime Minister is behaving increasingly like Catherine the Great and surrounding herself with favourites. If she cannot install them at the head of the relevant department, she puts them inside Number 10 and ignores the Departments altogether. ………It was one thing to staff No. 10 with bizarre interlopers from academia, such as Professor Walters, the Dr. Who of economics or Sir John Hoskyns, the rich man's Frances Morrell. It is fascinating to see how the right hon. Lady has begun to pluck people out of retirement. In diplomatic terms Sir Anthony (Parsons) is probably the George Smiley of the Foreign Office. Maybe he

is a double agent and works just as well for the Foreign Office as he does for her. I know that is the Foreign Secretary's hope. I wonder where the right hon. Lady will find the next of Smiley's people? Unfortunately, Sir Nico Henderson has already pre-empted the role of Sir Toby Esterhazy."

Everyone enjoyed the fun. Following on, Dr. David Owen begins by acknowleding that it would be churlish not to admit that the House had enjoyed the speech of the right hon. Member for Leeds.

Monetarism was a sore point with Healey:

"The right hon. Lady has been boasting in the last few days that in Ottawa she and Chancellor Schmidt found themselves both following middle of the road monetarist policies. I shall read not what he might have said to her, tired and late one evening in the log cabin when they were chatting together, but what he said when he gave an interview a fortnight ago to one of his newspapers – 'That West Germany

The Wit and Wisdom of Denis Healey

will not under any circumstances adopt a monetarist policy'."

Answering Mr. Norman Atkinson:

"I never used the word 'semantics'. I am not quite sure what it means. I said that there are as many types of monetarists as there are Christians. I said that I regarded the Leader of the Opposition as Torquemada in this instance."

As often, there is no answer to Healey's replies.

Getting out of a sticky point quickly when challenged by Mr. Lawson that he talks one way and acts in another regarding monetary policy he says:

"Let me help the right hon. Gentleman in his troubles. I am an unorthodox neo-Keynesian monetarist."

On Tory wets:

"However, the trouble is that people cannot hope for much from the Tory wets. As the Prime Minister said in one of her more elegant phrases, they 'lack guts and gumption'."

"Even the chairman of the Tory Party, Lord Thorneycroft, recently described himself as 'a reluctant example of rising damp'."

Putting a religious spin on his appraisal of an historical wonder he stated that in just two years Mr.Gorbachev transformed President Reagan and Prime Minister Thatcher from fanatical anti-Soviet crusaders into champions of détente and disarmament.

Healey says: "God moves in mysterious ways His wonders to perform and sometimes chooses unexpected vessels for His grace. The alchemy of history can change the basest metals into gold."

One of the best remembered incidents of his life as Chancellor happened on 28 September 1975 when on his way to an IMF meeting in Manila he turned at London Airport because he would have been out of telephone communication during a crisis with the falling pound. This simple visual memory from television coverage and his subsequent borrowing from the IMF gave his opponents opportunities for later barbs. It remained in people's memories when his later successes at the Treasury did not. Mrs. Thatcher, among others, took solace in mentioning it.

However, Healey managed to get the last laugh.

When an opponent, stepping high, unaware that Nemesis was at his heels, asked in 1990 if he felt a sense of shame about the time when, as Chancellor, he had to go cap in hand to the International Monetary Fund, Healey answered robustly:

> "To be quite honest I do not. I am often criticised for having gone to the IMF but let me give the Gentleman the facts. In 1976, I borrowed £2.5 billion from the IMF at an interest rate of between four and five percent; I paid it all back by 1979. Last year alone, this government borrowed £1.9 billion from the financial markets at interest rates four or five times as high. According to the Chancellor, this year they are borrowing £15 billion from the financial markets at 3.5 times higher than the rates I incurred.

I thank the hon. Gentleman for giving me the opportunity to say that. However, I confess I did slip the hon. Gentleman a pony, and he has performed the necessary service with exquisite aplomb."

In 1974 even in the midst of a long and serious discussion explaining the Defence Budget Healey could be lighthearted.

Coming to a point raised by Mr. Maud and noting his absence he says:

> "I am sorry that the hon. Member for Stratford-on-Avon has either slumped to the floor or has perhaps gone out for a cup of tea."

However this was anticipated and Mr. Horden answered:

> "My hon. Friend the Member for Stratford-on-Avon asked me to say, if the right hon. Gentleman referred to his remarks, that he is regrettably absent in Committee upstairs."

Healey answers: "Of course I accept that. I did not intend my bantering remarks to be taken as a serious rebuke."

On this same Budget he was able to get the better of his critics:

> "The judgement which I have made in my Budget is the median position of most commentators. Yesterday, of the three most expensive Sunday newspapers, one thought that I had been too deflationary, the second thought that I had been too inflationary and the third accompanied a sermon, in which its city editor claimed that tax avoidance was now a patriotic duty, with two articles, one taking each of the opposing views."

He often commented on the lack of attention paid by members of the House:

> "The Foreign Secretary is studiously avoiding listening to me, although I can see signs of anxiety on his face that suggest that he is still alive and well, and even living in London and sitting on the Government Front Bench."

Even in the most serious moments he could raise a smile.

In 1979 when the Labour government suffered defeat in a vote of no confidence and Healey was due to deliver his 15th Budget in five years he came to the House to deliver a Finance Bill instead, saying:

> "I confess that I feel a little like a man who turns up to play the leading role in opera and all they want him to do is to help them hold the scenery together."

Perhaps his most famous comment!

After disappointments with the results of a budget that was too harsh to business with its increased corporate taxes and having overestimated the ability of business to pay, Healey coined the cryptic phrase:

> "If you are in a hole stop digging."

He used this to good effect in later comments. In a debate on the budget and the economic situation in 1983 he says:

> "At present the Americans have adopted the first law of holes. I wish that the Government would adopt that law too. The first law of holes is that when someone is in one he stops digging."

In an address in the Lords in May 2005, Lord Newby uses Denis Healey's most quoted advice:

> "At every point he has failed to take the advice of his predecessor, the noble Lord Healey, when it comes to tax complexity. He knows that it is a bad thing in principle, but, unlike the noble Lord Healey, he has not realized that, when you are in a hole, you need to stop digging."

He was always in tune with the common culture.

On Tory proposals to bring the exiled rich back by lower taxes, he says:

> "If the top rate of income tax were fifty percent it would cost us four hundred million. That would mean getting eight thousand pop stars earning one hundred million a year back to Britain. Even if we could do it, the thought of eight thousand Bay City Rollers......" (laughter and applause)

On his defeat by Michael Foot for Leader of the Party his usual reply was in the words of an unsuccessful American candidate:

> "I would rather that people wonder why I am not president than why I am."

He showed no regrets saying that he was in politics "to do something rather than to be something". However, history has shown how catastrophic this choice was for Labour. Healey is acknowledged by many as the best leader Labour overlooked as explored fully in 'The Lost Leaders' by Edward Pearce.

Recognising the dangers inherent in the break up of the Soviet Union with the prospect of a sell off of nuclear weapons this dramatic image makes his comment memorable. It was also an astute forecast:

> "It is often said that it is not easy to turn an omelette back into eggs - Since perestroika began, the Soviet economy has followed a steady course downward, and there seems no prospect at the moment

of reversing it—the dangers of nuclear weapons being sold around the world as the system disintegrates - individuals and groups can buy weapons...."

1982/3 - On the government's attempts to weaken the Soviet Union by increasing its economic difficulties Healey comments on the US persuading its allies to embark on economic warfare against the Soviet Union in a concerted campaign to damage the Soviet economy

"....in the belief that thin Russians are in some sense less dangerous than fat Russians."

In 1983 speaking on what he called the idiocies of the common agricultural policy- he said:

"The Minister of Agriculture, Fisheries and Food announced yesterday that the European Commission is now selling 30,000 tonnes of butter, including British butter, to the Soviet Union with a subsidy of 47 pence per pound. The Russians will thus pay half the price that British housewives have to pay in British shops. I am forced once again to the conclusion that the common agricultural policy is a device invented by the Central Intelligence Agency of the United States of America to undermine the red army by pumping its veins full of cholesterol from cheap Common Market butter. It is impossible to find any other rational explanation for what Western Governments are tolerating."

Healey the scholar:

Of those who learned Shakespeare by heart, few could quote as effectively and wittily while on their feet. On the Canada Bill 1982 he points out:

"It is difficult to tread a proper path between the law's delay and the proud man's contumely."

This is a very useful tack for all politicians!

On the Falklands issue, when asked to repudiate extremely damaging remarks made by a Member of his Party when travelling to America to engage in discussion, Healey replies:

"It may be no surprise to the House to know that I have no personal responsibility for what is said by the right hon. Gentleman referred to."

On Bernard Levin the columnist:

When advised to read a comment by Bernard Levin, in The Times, to the effect that what his budget had done if offered by a public company would be referred to the D.P.P., Healey replied:

"I am not normally prepared to reveal my reading habits, but I follow Mr. Levin's articles from time to time and was delighted to discover the other day that his real trouble, according to him, is that he suffers from the death watch beetle."

On encouraging changes inside the Soviet Union since Mr. Gorbachev became General Secretary:

"....and I noticed this morning that even Mr. Bernard Levin had left his machine-gun post unmanned on the Golan Heights to express his views about what was happening in the Soviet Union and, very reluctantly, to speculate that just possibly the whole system is beginning to transform itself."

Again on Levin:

"Until the hon. and learned Gentleman made his entrance a moment ago, we never had such a din, such a monstrous cacophony, as we had last week. We even had that gargantuan economic, Bernard Levin squeaking away in the undergrowth like a demented vole."

On the withdrawal of 'HMS Endurance' from the Falklands, a typical tongue in cheek comment!

"Surely the Government put themselves in the situation in which they decided to withdraw 'HMS Endurance'. The only option open to them is to ask the Australian Government to allow 'HMS Invincible' to spend some time around the Falkland Islands on her way to serve with the Australian Navy."

On disarmament 1984, an up to date assessment:

"What must worry all people throughout the Western world is that technology is now moving at the speed of lightening and that diplomacy is moving with the stately majesty of a glacier. The responsibility for that must lie in part with Western governments, including Her Majesty's Government."

He continues with a statement that it is important to discuss East/ West relations more specifically asking Sir Geoffrey Howe about Mrs. Thatcher's visit to Hungary:

"Would the right hon. and learned Gentleman tell us a little about the implications.......Does he really believe that the Prime Minister's visit to Hungary will fulfil that need? Is it not rather like visiting the mayor of Reading because one does not want to talk to the Leader of the G.L.C?"

Regarding the cuts in spending in October, 1991 and the likely consequences he says:

"I belong to the same dwindling band as the Hon Member for East Leigh who fought in the last war because of the follies of the pre-war government."

On learning from the legacies of colonization and the ensuing instability:

"The end of the cold war has led to an explosion in nationalism which has created immense instability in what was once the Soviet empire…We should have been well prepared for that because the end of the British, French and Dutch empires produced the same instability in the third world, and that instability has lasted from 1945 to the present day (1991)."

In 1991 he gives this brief and memorable analysis of modern finance and economics:

"It has not been mentioned that information technology, combined with the abolition of exchange rate controls, has robbed all countries, which have abolished exchange rate controls and have information technology, of economic sovereignty. Money is now managed by a mafia of young lemmings, who send twenty times as much money across the foreign exchanges in search of speculative gain as is required to finance world trade in both services and industry. The young men on the financial markets determine exchange rates, and through exchange rates they determine interest rates. Through both they determine inflation and growth in all countries. That makes most of the argument about economics and monetary union almost irrelevant to the real world."

He could always open a new line of observation just for fun:

"Just to satisfy my hon. Friend the Member for Bolsover, (Mr. Skinner) let me say a word about the Prime Minister (John Major). I watched the right hon. Gentleman's face as his predecessor spoke this afternoon and I have never seen such inspissated gloom etched on a human visage in my life. When the right hon.

Member for Finchley (Mrs. Thatcher) said she planned to support him in the next election, he must have been reminded of Lenin's promise to support the social democrats as the rope supports the hanged man."

Mr. Skinner (the beast of Bolsover) and the Speaker were not above aiding and abetting in the fun.

In December 1975 during a debate on employment Mr. Healey said:

> "If my hon. Friend the Member for Bolsover (Mr. Skinner) would keep his trap shut, the whole House would be grateful."

Mr. Skinner: "On a point of order, Mr. Speaker was that a parliamentary expression?"

Mr. Speaker: "I do not think that asking an hon. Member to shut up is un-parliamentary. How it is precisely phrased is not a matter for the Chair.

Mr. Skinner: "Further to that point of order Mr. Speaker, I am getting more than a little concerned about the use of language in the House. No doubt you will have noticed yesterday that the Secretary of State for the Environment used the word 'codswallop'. Now the Chancellor of the Exchequer talks about keeping one's trap shut. I think that you should be doing something about this trend."

Mr. Speaker: "One of my difficulties is that when the Chancellor of the Exchequer is standing where he does at the Dispatch Box, I cannot see whether the hon. Gentleman's trap is shut or open."

Mr. Healey continues:

> "As I was saying before I was so agreeably interrupted I cannot forecast......"

In 1991 on John Major, he invents an imbroglio purely for fun:

> "All of us like the Prime Minister and it is difficult to be rude about him....I have not yet attempted it but I must confess that he reminds me of one of the most notable characters in current folklore...Charlie Brown in 'Peanuts'. You may remember Mr. Speaker, because I am sure that you are an avid follower of 'Peanuts', that Charlie Brown was once approached by Lucy...a

bossy little girl (Laughter). The parallel escapes me. Lucy asked Charlie to join her on an ocean cruise, so they got the boat and she took Charlie up to the sun deck and said to Charlie 'Now Charlie, there you will see a stack of deckchairs and you have to put your deckchair up…and Charlie, if you want to look backwards, you put it facing the stern of the boat'…which she obviously preferred herself 'but if you want to look forward into the future , you place it facing the prow of the boat. Now, Charlie' she said 'which way do you want your deckchair facing?' Charlie replied ….. so much like the Prime Minister 'I don't seem to be able to get my deckchair unfolded'."

On John Major's difficulties:

"I realize that if someone is driving a car, and sitting behind him is a lady with a handbag and a man with fangs, he may feel it wise to drive in the slow lane. My advice is that he should pull over into a lay-by, turf the others out and then hand the wheel to firmer and safer hands."

In a complaint about John Major's interview where he said that monetary union was 'spectacularly hypothetical' Denis Healey said:

"Somehow I wish the right hon. Gentleman had been gobsmacked at birth."

Nothing like a bit of exaggeration for effect:

On the many interruptions to his speech in the House of Commons:

"I do not think the opposition can ask me to go further now, particularly if hon. Members opposite want me to answer some of the forty nine questions which the right hon. Gentleman, the Member for Saffron Walden, asked yesterday."

Sir Geoffrey Howe answers aptly and with good reason:

"The right hon. Gentleman knows more about fatuity than most people."

On Southern Rhodesia 1991

He says he does not envy the hon. Gentleman who has to negotiate with Mr.

Smith on the termination of the unilateral declaration of independence. This has been found by many Ministers in the past to be "like trying to pick up mercury with knitting needles."

In Jan. 1972 on the Attorney General's (Sir Peter Rawlinson) comment that Africans were responding in normal political activity he points bluntly to the truth:

> "Of course I applaud the African response, but to claim that when the Africans respond and they are put into gaol, tear-gassed, shot and wounded, is normal political activity is a travesty of the facts."

Pointing up the robust/brutal reputation of one of his Labour colleagues:

On banking sector loans, he replies to Denis Skinner (the beast of Bolsover) "My hon. Friend, with whom on this series of issues I have long agreed, or he has agreed with me – I am not sure which is the more dangerous – is absolutely right."

At another point when asked to give way, Healey could turn the tables on his opponents, first saying "No", but on hon. Members shouting "Give way" he says:

> "Of course I shall give way, but I do not believe in giving way every three seconds; otherwise I might prevent my hon. Friend from making the speech that he intends to make."

Implying that he is not asking for too much and an excuse for a joke:

Healey: "Will the Chancellor give us an imprecise estimate?

Geoffrey Howe got round to them a trifle nervously I thought after ploughing through a tedious and tendentious farrago of moth eaten cuttings presented to him by the Conservative research department .That part of his speech was rather like being savaged by a dead sheep."

The following, again, shows some indulgence by the Speaker of the House of Commons:

Tim Eggar rose and Denis Healey said: "Oh, sit down."

On a point of order, Mr. Eggar asked if it was in order for Denis Healey to refer to hon. Members in that way.

The Deputy Speaker: "Unusual, I would say."

He was adept at spotting humour in the words of others, now heightened in retrospect. No one was too clever or erudite to escape Healey's wit.

In May 1980 he quotes what the Secretary of State for Industry (Sir Keith Joseph) said to the Conservative Conference in 1973 when, Healey says, he was appealing simply to the Conservatives' sense of political interest.   Healey continues:

> "I quote the right hon. Gentleman's words because they are well constructed and give a revealing insight into the general attitude of intelligent Conservatives to these problems.   The right hon. Gentleman said: 'Withdrawing a bone from a dog's mouth has its difficulty, particularly when the dog has a wife and children.   This conference would be the first to howl if we really did have pictures on television of children going hungry for lack of benefits – perhaps because their striking fathers

were on low pay and had not been able to save, perhaps even because their striking fathers had not made the necessary arrangements for saving for the purpose. But this Conference would object strongly if children were shown going without food.'

With sardonic mirth Healey adds: "I hope the Conservative Party is still capable of listening to appeals of this type."

Now and again Healey was the 'parfit gentle knight':

When Mrs. Thatcher, as Prime Minister, was ousted from the Leadership by the somewhat cruel tactics of members of her own Party, Healey spoke with some feeling showing his traits of innate chivalry:

"I have been privileged to be drawn in debate against the Prime Minister for some 16 years now, since she was a junior Treasury spokesman - and, if I may say so, a very able one. For anyone who has watched her for so long, it is a moving experience to see her leaving her position in such circumstances. I must confess that, during the Prime Minister's Question time and much of her speech in this debate, I thought that she showed her finest qualities and I listened to her with sympathy and admiration. She has guts, and she has a degree of determination to which I fear that none of those who are now challenging her can lay claim. I agree very much with the right hon. Member for Castle Point on that point: she has guts."

Whatever the subject matter he could attack it in a jovial light.

Continuing on disloyalty to Mrs. Thatcher within the Conservative Party:

"Many of us remember with affection the late Lord Kilmuir – previously Sir David Maxwell Fyfe - of whom it was once said, 'There is nothing more like death in life than Sir David Maxwell Fyfe'......When he went to the Lords, he told a wondering world that loyalty was the Conservative Party's secret weapon. The trouble is that, as has been shown during recent weeks, the loyalty of the Tory party is similar to that of Colonel Nasser's generals, of whom it was said that they would be 1,000 percent loyal until the day treachery arrived. Now, it could be more fairly said that disloyalty is the Conservative party's public weapon. It has been a distasteful fight during the past few days."

Regarding property speculators, Healey would be useful to-day.

Commenting on Lord Carrington's having made ten million profit by selling land at thirty to sixty times its price as agricultural land Healey promised to "squeeze the property speculators until the pips squeak".

He also promised to "wring the neck of the Housing Finance Act".

The impressionist Mike Yarwood coined for him the catchphrase "Silly Billy", which he adopted and used frequently. It somehow suited his jovial personality.

He seemed to inspire wit in others. The otherwise dry Harold Wilson sums him up as follows:

"He is a strange person. When he was at Oxford he was a Communist. Then friends took him in hand, sent him to the Rand Corporation of America, where he was brainwashed and came back very right wing. But his method of thinking was still what it had been, in other words, the absolute certainty that he was right and everybody else was wrong, and not merely wrong through not knowing the proper answers, but wrong through malice..... But he was a strong colleague and much respected."

Some of his opponents set a trap for themselves:

When he made mention of Sir Ian Gilmour's "passion", Sir Ian protested:

> "I am sorry to complain again about the right hon. Gentleman's language, but I think that "passion" is a rather strong word to use as far as I am concerned.

Healey answered: "I apologise to the right hon. Gentleman. I should not have described his pallid languor as passion. Perhaps the word I should have used was velleity."

A little learning is a dangerous thing when attacking Denis Healey.

The proud and confident Alan Clark (of the Diaries) was no match for Healey when he made some barbed comments on his inconsistencies. Healey answers with aplomb:

> "No one who has attended our debates will be surprised that the hon. Gentleman has no sense of history and no political memory."

He then goes on to remind him of the decisions by NATO governments in 1979. He finishes with a flourish:

> "I hope that the hon. Gentleman will not interrupt again, especially with a silly preamble, when he has shown himself so vulnerable."

He could always turn the tables on others when they made a reply that he himself often got away with.

In a debate on Poland/ war/ arms control when Douglas Hurd interrupts with one word, "Nonsense" Healey replies:

"The right hon. Gentleman had very little to say about it. Anyone can verify that by reading Hansard to-morrow."

In a debate on the Brandt report, commenting on Sir Ian Gilmour's speech he complains that the government had no sense of the urgency needed to help the poorer nations.

"When I listened to the right hon. Gentleman, I could not help remembering the story about the Highlander who was asked what the word in the highlands was for mañana. He said I do not think we have a word in our part of Scotland that quite conveys that sense of urgency."

On riots/crime/unemployment in 1981 he said:

"The Chief Secretary (the right hon. Leon Brittan) had inverted the law of gravity and had propounded the superb economic truism that what comes down must go up. That was the basis of his belief that the economy was about to recover."

On a reversal of policies:

"The Chancellor of the Exchequer finally aligned himself with the European critics of high interest rate policies in the United States. It is a wonderful example of Satan rebuking sin, but is welcome none the less."

Likewise in 1956 he had a somewhat hopeful outlook on the duty of the United Nations to co-operate in trying to create order.

Healey answers an opponent:

"I believe we do have an opportunity now, which we may not have had earlier, for making a reality of the United Nations. I hope that the right hon. Gentleman will not try to take credit for this – it would be like Al Capone taking credit for improving the efficiency of the Chicago police."

On the lack of political co-operation in the European Community in 1981:

"Will the Lord Privy Seal confirm that the list of the Government's achievements during their presidency will be contained on the back of a very small stamp …….no progress on reforming budgetary arrangement, the common agricultural policy or the finance policy."

He could capture a visual likeness with apt expression.

In a debate on South Georgia and the Falklands:

"The right hon. Member for Down (Enoch Powell) expressed very strongly a different view. He suggested that any compromise on this issue would be wholly unacceptable, and he put the case with his usual glittering and icy logic which is a wonderful machine for dazzling the groundlings."

In response to some very detailed nitpicking from Enoch Powell, Healey manages to get the upper hand as usual. He responds:

"When I was in Canberra last year I discovered that when the right hon. Member for Wolverhampton South West(Enoch Powell) was teaching Greek at the university there, he had the nickname 'textual pervert', the reason being that he was liable to base extraordinary fantastic conclusions on some very simple use of words."

He had a superb command of English and perfect timing.

When asked by the Secretary of State for Wales (Mr. Nicholas Edwards) to withdraw the nonsense he had just uttered, Denis Healey replied:

"I hope the right hon. Gentleman will withdraw that silly and otiose intervention."

Urbane and effective, he was a master of the understatement as well as the robust observation:

"As an honest and dispassionate observer, I think you will have been witness, Mr. Speaker, that I have given way a good deal already, and I should like an opportunity to finish my speech."

In a debate on privatization in the Health Service:

"So far the Government have made an exception only of the Armed Forces, but given a chance the Prime Minister will be handing over Defence in the next Government, or the one after that, to the Mafia and the Kray brothers."

In Oct 1982, as always, on the ball when finance was under discussion:

"The medium-term financial strategy was another invention of the Secretary of State for Energy, who was then the right hon. Member for Blaby (Mr. Lawson). He is the man who gave us the Lawson index and the monetarist mumbo-jumbo which was interred the other day by the Bank of England."

Some nostalgia in a debate on the economy in 1983:

"For me there is an element of nostalgia to which the Chancellor referred in this debate. It is some time since he and I confronted one another across the Dispatch Box. We are both older now than we were. I must say that, on this occasion, I feel a little more as if I was being nibbled by a hearthrug."

On Mrs. Thatcher's adopting royal airs by using the royal "we":

"When she arrived back from her visit to the Falklands she joined Queen Victoria in her regal pantheon by saying:

'We are not impressed by the behaviour of the markets'."

At another point he says that she scattered the word "we" like confetti when referring to "her own royal personage".

In 1983, contrasting Mrs. Thatcher with Conservatives such as Lord Shaftesbury and Benjamin Disraeli he says: "the Prime Minister and the secretary of State for employment are the Gradgrind and Bounderby of modern Britain, and they glory in it."

Commenting in 1983 that sterling had fallen by thirteen percent in six months he says:

"…the last time sterling fell, the Chancellor of the Exchequer intervened. He took advantage of the Prime Minister's absence in the Falkland Islands to raise interest rates in order to break sterling's fall."

Sir Stanley Orme interrupts: "Where is the Prime Minister?"

Healey answers: "I do not know. If she stays out much longer the Chancellor may raise interest rates again and that would be terrifying for us all."

Never lost for a witty reply –

On the Brandt Commission report he said of the Chancellor of the Exchequer:

> "However, I was not clear whether in his speech to the Bow Group he was a wet in dry clothing or perhaps a dry in a wet blanket."

When Eric Deakins complained that there was no Treasury representative on the Government Front Bench, nor a representative from the Department of Trade saying that this pointed up the difference in the seriousness that the two parties view the problem of the world's poor, Healey answered:

> "My hon. Friend may be right but there is another possible explanation. It is possible that all the Treasury Ministers have departed to the central courtyard off

Great George Street to attend a ritual hari-kari of the official who gave the Foreign Secretary the figures that the Treasury has previously refused to give the House."

Healey, a fluent Italian speaker cannot resist a quip that we can all appreciate.

He mentions the Prime Minister "on the eve of a visit to Moscow in which we assume that she was hoping to cut what the Italians call 'una bella figura'."

An April Fool's Day joke:

On the softening relations between East and West Healey quotes an April Fool's Day joke from the Daily Mirror:

"The spring-like pictures also show why Mrs. Thatcher refused to let her husband Denis accompany her on this historic visit. For photographer Ken George and I witnessed the Prime Minister strolling arm-in- arm with Mr. Gorbachev, pausing to kiss and cuddle him and even tickle him under the chin like some flirty schoolgirl. Romance, April style, was clearly in the air."

Healey sums it up: "One touch of Venus transformed the iron lady into Lola Montez."

He says Mr. Gorbachev won hands down. He converted her lock, stock and barrel. "As Julius Caesar nearly wrote - she came, she saw, he conquered."

Healey usually enjoyed a barb directed at the great and good.

Agreeing that it was a worthwhile debate on the Grenada invasion……

> "From the right hon. Member for Down South (Mr. Enoch Powell) we had his familiar impersonation of General de Gaulle, and there was an equally familiar performance from the right hon. Member for Chelmsford (Mr. St. John-Stevas) as Obadiah Slope."

He was always able to debunk the officious.

As an ex-Secretary of State for Defence he was told that the configuration of the Polaris was the most jealously guarded secret in his possession. However, he writes that on his next visit to New York he was able to buy for his children a scale model of the Polaris submarine, produced by the Metal Toy Company.

He could say this again!

"It is such an unfamiliar experience for me to be accused of ambiguity that I misunderstood Mr. Johnson. I am puzzled as to what the right hon. Gentleman thinks. He said that he was very keen on annual reports, but also that he was not."

On South Africa:

"The Prime Minister has infuriated blacks and whites alike by her behaviour. How typical of her, that she should now be in New York to lecture President Reagan on how to make friends and influence people."

Throughout his political career he could always cope with the demands of the House:

"I shall give way regularly because I enjoy interventions and enjoy even more replying to them. However, Mr. Speaker, you have asked me not to waste time, so I shall continue."

When interrupted on a statement that the Royal Air Force Phantoms would be the most advanced type for another decade: (an hon. Member: 'All two of them') Healey continues:

"I wish the idiot who made that remark would stand up and reveal himself to the House."

He often used the anti-climax for effect, as follows on foreign affairs:

"The Foreign Secretary made a wide ranging speech in which he covered everything from the nuclear holocaust until he reached his crescendo on illegal parking. Nevertheless he rightly left some important issues - including one of the most difficult - to his hon. Friend the Minister of State. I was glad to note that there was a certain amount of traffic between the Front Bench and the civil servants' Box immediately following the handing over of that poisoned chalice."

On major issues he did not suffer fools gladly:

"May I congratulate the Foreign Secretary on the penetrating and comprehensive critique of the Star Wars programme that he made the other day, and on provoking an alarming outburst of hysteria from the editor of 'The Times'. President Reagan said he was ready to consider a ban or moratorium on tests of anti- satellite weapons whereas the Foreign Secretary said that the future is now control of chemical weapons…..."

He shared his sense of humour with others and this appears in his own writings.

He says that Mountbatten loved to tell the story of a Conservative canvasser at Broadlands to whom he opened the door during the general election of 1945. "I'm Labour myself," he told her, "but I think my butler votes Tory."

He gives a lesson on how to interpret political speech:

"Those of us who have some experience of this matter will know that when two countries fail to reach agreement on anything their talks are described as 'full and frank', but the word friendly is not added. On this occasion the talks were described by the Americans as 'direct and even blunt'. By that I would suggest that there was a flaming row."

He could go from the sublime to the ridiculous with ease and was always keen to add to or correct another's joke.

Colonel Tufton Beamish Lewes tells a joke as follows:

"I remember as a small child – and others will as well – asking a rather silly question. I asked 'what is it that goes ninety-nine bonk?' The answer used to be, 'a centipede'."

Healey corrects: "A centipede with a wooden leg."

Lastly, a compliment with a hint of a smile, from Gordon Brown:

In 2007, responding to an accusation of being dull Gordon Brown answers:

"Well I cannot sing or play the piano like Denis Healey" adding that treasury statements are inherently dry.

Time is now proving that he was a visionary and a man of learning with a deep knowledge of foreign affairs. We can still learn from his wisdom and expertise. The following words of wisdom should be written large for present day politicians.

On the Middle East, when the Jordanian Government expelled the Palestinians into Lebanon, and on instability in the Lebanon:

> "To attempt to create a Christian banana republic, kept alive by wealthy European tourists as an Israeli satellite is doomed to disaster."

On terrorism: (1986)

> "Britain has a longer experience of terrorism than any other country, going back to colonial days. Even in my lifetime, we have fought terrorism in India, Palestine, Malaya, Cyprus and Kenya, and we are fighting it today in Northern Ireland. In this long experience of terrorism, we have learnt three

lessons. The first is that the indiscriminate use of force in a campaign against terrorism simply creates more terrorists. It is a major objective of terrorists to compel the legal authorities to use excessive force against them. We have also learnt that there are only two answers to terrorism. The first is painstaking police work supported by effective intelligence, combined with the protection of the most vulnerable targets. The second is political action to remove the grievances which are the breeding ground for terrorism. If we can do that, we have at best succeeded in converting terrorists into statesmen – for example, Nehru, Makarios, Kenyatta, and Begin…"

Wisdom on Arab nationalism, (1958) voiced almost fifty years ahead of other statesmen:

Healey said that it was "a dictum of Lenin that Russian success would be assured if Russia could achieve an alliance between Soviet Communism and Asian Nationalism" mentioning people who worked for the oil companies, Foreign Office or who served in the army, "and I have yet to meet anyone actually working at the present time in the Middle East who believes that it is possible to beat Arab nationalism."

In June 1982 in a debate on the Middle East he warns again, almost twenty years before the Western World woke up:

"I think probably that one of the biggest mistakes that the Western World has made in approaching these problems in the last few years is to underestimate the importance of the new theocratic movement in the Muslim world. This new type of Muslim fundamentalism is now as powerful on the Indian sub-continent as it is in the Middle East itself. It is a fundamentalism that has sent men riding bicycles into mine fields shouting 'God is great'. None of us can remember except from history books, the power of this type of Muslim fundamentalism when it last conquered the Middle East, much of India and half of Europe. But that power is a reality today. Dealing with it is one of the most difficult problems that will face all other Governments in the world, Western or Communist.

If Iraq, which has a very large majority of Shi'ites in its population were to join Iran.....that would form a block of people controlling the movement of oil."

His words of wisdom on our dependence on Gulf oil are still relevant:

"The Gulf will remain unstable however the crisis is resolved, and there is an overwhelming case for reducing the West's dependence on oil from the Gulf. American experts have calculated that if America had maintained the energy-saving programmes that it followed between 1977 and 1985, it would now be totally independent of Gulf oil. If the Americans taxed gasoline to the level at which we tax it here, it would solve their budget problem and encourage the use of smaller cars. If Americans simply replaced their older cars that now do only 19 miles to the gallon with some that do 29 miles to the gallon, it would have no use of Gulf oil."

Again in January 1991 words on the first Gulf war that could inform present decisions:

"When I consider that we are contemplating a war without formal agreement that the Saudis and the Muslim contingents will join in I feel very much like the German admiral who, when the multilateral force was explained to him some time ago, replied: 'I would rather swim'."

Denis Healey, a splendid orator, a rough, tough yet genial debater, a well travelled expert on foreign affairs is one of our great wits.

Acknowledgements

Hansard: Reproduced by permission of the Controller of Her Majesty's Stationery Office.

Healey, Denis, The Time of My Life (Michael Joseph, 1989)

Healey, Edna, Part of the Pattern, Memoirs of a Wife at Westminster (Headline Review, 2006) Reproduced by permission of Headline Publishing Group LTD

Labour Party Conference Report 1952

Wilson, Harold, Memoirs - The Making of a Prime Minister (Weidenfeld and Nicholson and Michael Joseph 1986)

EILEEN METCALFE, née Gallen, a teacher, schools inspector and educational consultant was born in Co. Donegal, Eire. She lives in Welchtown, Co. Donegal and in Leeds.

Printed in the United Kingdom
by Lightning Source UK Ltd.
125710UK00001B/12/A